CW00924429

The Beginner's Guide to Gold and Silver Scrap

Basic Fundamentals for Buying Scrap Precious Metals

V Alexander Cullen

From the Author of Pawnbrokers Handbook

The Beginner's Guide to Gold and Silver Scrap:
Basic Fundamentals for Buying Scrap Precious
Metals
By V. Alexander Cullen
Copyright © 2013 by V. Alexander Cullen

This book is dedicated to my sweet spouse Lynn.

Cover Photography by L. D. Cullen

2

Contents

• •

Introduction

This is the third book I have written that covers the subject of buying scrap gold and silver. This will be the final book I write on this subject. My intention is make it as short and simple as possible. My goal is to educate the reader with the basics of buying scrap gold and silver. My first book, "Pawnbrokers Handbook" is intended to train Pawnbrokers. Buying Jewelry, Scrap Gold and Silver is an important part of that business. My second book "Gold and Silver Scrap Dealers Handbook" is intended for those who don't want to be Pawnbrokers but do want to be licensed store front dealers and are primarily interested in buying jewelry, gold, silver, coins and flatware for retail sales as well as scrap. It goes into greater detail about the retail sale and appraisal of fine jewelry. Most of the information in that book was taken directly from the previous one. This book is intended for those who are only interested in the basic metals in scrap gold and silver objects, how to test and weigh them and make a profit from their labors. Diamonds and other gemstones can also be part of these objects so I will briefly cover the subject of gemstones so the reader will be able to reap any additional rewards that might be available. There is a market for used diamonds and colored gemstones in the jewelry repair trade. The basics never change and most of the knowledge you find in this book comes directly from my previous two books. I did receive some criticism from readers about dated information in both of my previous books. When I wrote "Pawnbrokers Handbook" the price of gold was around $300 per ounce and silver was about $6 per ounce. Today, as I write this book, the price for gold in US dollars on the

5

first London Fix is just under $1600 per troy ounce and silver is just under $30 per troy ounce. It is, of course, impossible to change the content of a book once it is published therefore I will use the V Alexander Cullen gold fix price of $1000 US dollars per troy ounce and $30 US dollars for silver. The reader must adjust the formulas in the following pages to the current price for gold and silver and for their nation's currency.

I have been a "Gold Bug" for many years and I believe that the price of gold will go much higher in the future. Because the world is on the dollar standard, our Federal Reserve System has been able to print as many dollars as it wants and call it "Quantitative Easing". We had QE1, QE2 and lately QE3. The word I would use for this practice is "inflation". Will we see QE4, QE5, QE6, etc? The price of gold jumped this morning because politicians in tiny little Cyprus decided to confiscate up to 10 percent of all the bank deposits of all its citizens. Multiply what is happening in Cyprus by 100 and that may be the future for us all. I am not a prophet but I can see the cost of everything going up. One of the reasons I have bought scrap gold and silver is to have it converted into coins as a hedge against inflation. I am usually able to acquire these coins for about half as much as I would if I bought them through a dealer. Most refiners will exchange scrap precious metals for minted bullion coins. I see the world's financial system teetering on the edge of a deep hole and if it falls I want to have some cold hard cash, real money, gold and silver to cushion the blow.

In the absence of the gold standard, there is no way to protect savings from confiscation through inflation. There is no safe store of value.
Alan Greenspan

Chapter 1

•••••••••••••••••••••••••

Tools and Basics

"The desire of gold is not for gold. It is for the means of freedom and benefit."
— *Ralph Waldo Emerson*

TOOLS OF THE TRADE

To buy scrap gold and silver you will need to weigh it and determine the gold or silver content of the item. A good scale is a necessity. If you want to buy precious metals as a licensed dealer you will need a scale that is legal for trade and can be certified by your State Bureau of Weights and Measures. They should be NTEP certified. New ones start around $300 and you can find a large selection by doing an internet search. If you don't plan to go into business but just want trade with scrap gold and silver as a "hobby" then there are much cheaper alternatives. I still have my old Ohaus balance scales. They work every time even without electricity.

The next thing you will need is a system to test metals. After years of experience I can look at an item and tell whether it is fake or not with at least a 95% accuracy. If I have any doubts I will use a little nitric acid. Most people rely on a Touch Stone which are nondestructive and 98% accurate. The other option is an electronic pen which is easy to use but slightly less accurate at about 92%. Touch Stones work by rubbing the item on a stone and putting acid on the mark. A color comparison can then be done to determine the Karat of the item. Electronic pens will use a chemical gel to test the conductivity of the item. These have become much more sophisticated than they were when they first came out. There is even one that will work with an Android Smartphone. The only other practical nondestructive option is an X-ray Fluorescence machine. These are extremely accurate but are very expensive. If you decide to start with a touch stone kit, get one that includes the test acids for silver and platinum also. I have seen complete testing kits online that include everything you need to get started including scale, loupe, touch stone, acids, diamond tester and a small silver bar to practice on, all for $60.

Unless you have really exceptional eyesight you will need magnification to see markings on items. I recommend a 10X jeweler's loupe. Optional tools will be necessary if you want to test diamonds and dismount them or other stones for their scrap values.

Electronic diamond tester

Accurate diamond gauge

Moe diamond gauge and calculator

Ring clamp

Needle-nose pliers

Jeweler's saw and blades

The idea is to save any stones you can remove from settings to sell for extra income.

10

Anyone, with a little knowledge and a few tools, can make good money buying scrap gold and silver. Any one already in business can supplement that business buying scrap gold and silver. You can buy scrap gold and silver as a "side business" if you are employed by someone else. It is a great way to supplement a retirement income. Anyone can buy precious metals scrap but some states do require licensing. The latest fad is to have "Gold Buying Parties". People invite friends, relatives, coworkers and neighbors to clean out their junk drawers and jewelry boxes for any items that might have gold or silver in them. They will come to the sponsor's home and sell their unwanted items for cash. You can have business cards made that explain what kind of items you are looking for and pass them out to any likely prospect. The gold and silver you buy as scrap can be sold to a refiner for cash or you can take payment in freshly minted gold and silver bullion coins for your own collection.

SILVER JEWELRY

When I wrote "Pawnbroker's Handbook" many years ago, silver stayed in the $4 to $6 per ounce range. Today it is hovering around $30 per ounce. At those prices, silver jewelry is more attractive to buy for scrap. It takes a lot of silver jewelry to be worth much though. Silver jewelry is usually marked "Sterling" or "925" and is 92.5% pure silver. If spot silver is $30 per ounce, there is $27.75 pure silver per ounce of "Sterling". If you divide that by 20 pennyweights per Troy ounce, then it's $1.39 per pennyweight pure silver value. I would offer about 70 cents per pennyweight. Large chains, heavy rings or a pile of smaller pieces can be worth dealing with. Most stones mounted in silver have little value. Turquoise is common and not worth much but there are some silver jewelry by famous artisans that can be quite valuable. Before you send a piece off to be melted it is a good

12

idea to research any unusual pieces especially if they have unusual markings or hallmarks. Coins, flatware and hollowware are the best bet to buy silver in bulk. The best thing about silver is that is still affordable by the average person and if you do make a mistake when you buy it you are less likely to suffer great loss.

SILVER COINS

The value of silver has risen by seven and half times since "Pawnbrokers Handbook" was published and a pre-1965 US silver half dollar which had $1.45 worth of silver 20 years ago now has about $10.88 worth of silver with spot prices at $30 per ounce. I believe that silver has a tremendous upside potential. I can still remember my father buying silver like mad in his pawn shop when silver was $50 per ounce in the late seventies and early eighties. People were cashing in everything they could find with silver in it including grandma's silverware and grandpa's moustache cup. Gold was around $800 per ounce and Dad was shipping scrap metals to the refiner at least once per week.

Coins can be a very profitable part of the scrap buying business. A cull is a coin that is good only for its silver value. These coins are usually severely worn, but you will still be able to recognize them as U.S. coins. They may even have dates that are readable. These coins are traded in commodity markets by the bag and the half bag. A bag contains$1,000 face value worth of U.S. minted pre-1965 silver coins. They can be mixed denominations or of one denomination. Although most of the coins I see are culls, I do get some nice collector's pieces, mint sets, slabs, and complete collections.

It takes years of study and practice to become a certified numismatist who can professionally grade coins, and I cannot tell you everything about coins in this chapter. I can give you a few basics, but if you are not knowledgeable about this subject, it would be in your best interest to learn more.

There are two ways to value coins. One is by their silver value, and the other is by their collector value. Try to buy coins based on their silver content only. If the coins you are dealing with are of better grades, then you must figure out the collector value, which means you must grade them to the best of your ability. One of the books I use is the Handbook of United States Coins by R.S. Yeoman, which lists dealer's buying prices. This and every good coin book has a section on how to grade coins. I find myself reading this section every time I look up a coin to refresh my memory. Most of the values are based not only on the amount of wear to the high points of the coin, but also on its date, where it was minted, and the number of coins minted in that batch. I see very few coins that are uncirculated, and most are valued at the lower to middle end of the scale. There is also a chart in the back of Yeoman's book that shows the bullion value for each type of coin. Using this chart, you can figure out the silver value for any U.S. coin. For example, if the spot price of silver is $30 per ounce, a pre-1965 silver half-dollar, which has about 1/3 ounce of silver in it, would be worth about $10. I would offer $5 to $7 per half dollar coin to buy them. Most US silver coins are about 90% silver and are very easy to sell. Pre-1965 US silver coins are always in demand and consequentially you usually have to pay close to spot price to get them. If you have internet access, there are several good melt value calculators on the web such as; http://www.usacoinbook.com/coin-melt-values/calculators/silver/

Here is another for Canadian coins; http://coinapps.com/silver/coin/canadian/calculator/

GOLD COINS

Just like silver coins, gold coins have a numismatic value as well as bullion value. Gold coins are always in heavy demand and the competition to buy them can be intense. I can usually buy average circulated gold coins and bullion coins like American Eagles, Krugerrands, British Sovereigns and Canadian Maple Leafs for 80 to 90 percent of spot price. If the government ever decided to confiscate gold bullion like Franklin Roosevelt did in 1933, you might be able hold on to these as a "Coin Collection", maybe.

http://www.the-privateer.com/1933-gold-confiscation.html

I try to hold these when I can get them.

The coin books mentioned earlier and the online melt value calculators will give you the current metal value for these coins

SILVERWARE

Silver flatware and hollowware are always a good source for scrap silver. They must, of course, be solid silver, because silver-plated items aren't worth much. I always value silverware by the actual silver content in the piece. I will weigh it on my scale and estimate how much pure silver is in it. If I'm weighing a set of flatware, I will take each piece from a setting and weigh it, then multiply their weights by the number of settings there are. Large pieces of hollowware are sometimes too big to fit on my scale, so I must guess at the weight. Once I figure out the weight in troy ounces, I multiply this by the current spot price per ounce for pure silver. Just like sterling jewelry, most silverware is 92.5% pure silver. There are exceptions and I have seen silverware marked as "coin" silver which is 90% pure silver. When buying Sterling I must adjust the spot price of silver by 92.5 percent. For example, if the spot price for silver is $30 per ounce, silverware is worth $27.75 per ounce. I would offer $15 to $22 per ounce (66% spot price maximum). The Smelter will want to make a profit of 5 to 10 % also. I have seen complete 12 place setting sterling flatware sets weighing 40 or 50 ounces. Do beware of the knives as they almost always have hollow handles and steel blades. I would make every effort to sell any silverware you have acquired as scrap to folks who are willing to pay you a premium over scrap for these items to use or sell as silverware. Antique shops and Pawnshops can be a good place to do this. I have sold a lot of flatware and hollowware for double or triple the melt value, even more for extremely rare pieces. I always do some research before I send silverware off to be melted to see if there may be a better profit by selling it as is.

JEWELRY

As a scrap buyer you come across all types

of gold objects and a lot of them will have some type of precious or semiprecious jewel in them. For your benefit, you should consider diamonds to be precious stones; rubies, sapphires and emeralds to be semiprecious; and most everything else as weight to be removed or adjusted for.

Learn all you can about diamonds, gems, and gold. Many of the items you buy for scrap can be cleaned and repaired to be sold wholesale or retail. I have bought many items that required very little work to make them look like new and then sold them as jewelry. I am able to fix and polish jewelry myself but if you develop a relationship with a local jeweler you can have items which have potential for resale, polished and cleaned. He may even want to buy them from you to supplement his shop inventory. I have sold lots of scrap at better than current spot price to jewelers who make their own jewelry. They especially like old wedding bands which are perfect to cut up to size

20

other rings or to melt for castings. Many of the mounted stones in the items I buy for scrap are also saleable. Large diamonds have been regularly offered to me. Unlike gold and silver which can easily be evaluated for weight and content, diamonds are harder to judge. The diamond market is fickle and the scrap value of stones smaller than ½ carat crashed a few years ago. Even stones larger than ½ carat are worth less than they were 10 years ago. Be careful when investing in diamonds. Jewelers are still buying small diamonds and other stones for repairs but when they can buy new ones cheaply, they want to pay even less for used ones. I recommend buying jewelry with stones mounted mainly for the gold or silver content and if the piece looks like it could be resold as jewelry then pay a small premium for the value of the stone(s) and the value of the labor to mount it. I have seen many large semi-precious colored stones mounted in rings, pendants and pins that were as heavy as, or heavier than the mounting they came in. In most cases, I will discount what I will pay for the scrap value of the item, if there is such a stone in it, to compensate for the weight of the stone.

On very rare occasions, a platinum item will show up. Most of the platinum pieces I've seen are marked as 90% platinum. Platinum jewelry is usually the finest quality money can buy. If you can buy it for scrap prices try to buy it at the same ratio as gold or silver, about half of spot. Any platinum jewelry that is salvageable as jewelry will bring a premium price for resale. Most of the platinum jewelry I have come across is antique and estate pieces.

Other Objects

About the only other objects you will see is the occasional watch case and dental gold. There are a lot of gold plated watches out there so test them thoroughly. Most folks won't let you tear apart their watches but I get some that are broken and beyond repair that I can pull the guts out and the crystals off to get an accurate weight. I see a lot of Ladies watches that have gold cases. To weigh a watch accurately on the scales it will have to be stripped to the bare case.

Dental gold is usually in the form of gold teeth which is normally about 16K. For accurate weight I always ask the owner to make sure there isn't any leftover tooth material inside the object.

"[Gold] gets dug out of the ground in Africa, or someplace. Then we melt it down, dig another hole, bury it again and pay people to stand around guarding it. It has no utility. Anyone watching from Mars would be scratching their head."
— Warren Buffett

Chapter 2

....

Tricks of the Trade

"The road to hell isn't paved with gold, it's paved with faith. Faith in a dollar that's backed by a belief that people have faith in other people's belief in it."
— Jarod Kintz, *This Book is Not for Sale*

I still have the Ohaus triple beam scales that I started out with many years ago. They still work perfectly but are slow and tedious to use. I've been spoiled since I acquired my digital scales. It's nice to have an instant reading of weight without changing little weights and sliding little scales and reading hash marks to get an exact measurement. A good quality digital scale is truly an asset.

As far as which weight system to use, I

recommend that you use troy. I was trained in the troy system, and I don't care much for gram measurements. Gold is always traded in the world markets in troy ounces. Sometimes you may have to convert to gram weight for your customers, but digital scales can easily do this, which is another good reason to own one. Some scrap buyers buy and sell by gram weight but I believe in Troy weight. Here are some basics:

One troy pound = 12 troy ounces

One troy ounce = 20 pennyweight (dwt)

One pennyweight = 24 grains

15.43 grains = one gram (gm)

One gram = 1.6 pennyweight (approx.)

31.1 grams = one troy ounce

The Spot Market

If you want to be a successful Scrap Buyer, you will need to follow the price of gold carefully. The London market sets the daily price per troy ounce for precious metals in the world markets. This is referred to as the London "fix" and it is done twice a day. This price is for the spot market, which means this is the price you will pay if you take possession of the metals that day. This daily price quote is reported on radio and television financial programs and is published in the newspaper under metal commodities.

You can also follow it online or on a Smartphone App. These quotes will determine what you should pay and, to some extent, what you can sell your scrap metals and retail/wholesale jewelry for. Though metals are traded on the market in troy ounces, the main unit of measurement you need to be concerned about is the pennyweight. Almost all the buying and selling of Precious Metals you do will be done by pennyweight.

How Much to Pay for Gold

How much you pay for gold should be determined more by what you can scrap it for and less by what you think you may be able to retail it for as jewelry. It's true I will pay more for a nice resalable piece of jewelry than a piece that is good only for scrap, but I always pay less than gold value at the current market rate. To figure out the gold value for a specific piece of jewelry, you must begin by looking at the current market price. For example, if the current market price is $1000 per troy ounce, you must divide by 20 to get the price per pennyweight (dwt), which is $50. You should consider the profit margin of the refiner to whom you will sell it. Most refiners will pay at least 95 percent of spot price for a 5 percent profit margin. (The amount will vary according to the amount you scrap, and there are sometimes other fees involved.) So

$50 per pennyweight multiplied by 95 percent is $47.50. This is what you can realistically expect to sell gold for in the spot market on this particular day. You must also figure that on the day you actually sell your gold, the price may have changed. What will the price be tomorrow? If I were able to predict the answer to that question, I could be a Billionaire.

The price of gold fluctuates due to the influence of many different forces. Sometimes emotion or panic in world markets, political upheavals, and wars can affect prices. A strike in a gold-producing state like South Africa or a shooting war in an oil producing state like Kuwait will cause gold prices to go up. A big sell-off of gold by Russia or a large bank will cause gold prices to go down. Gold has always been used as a hedge against inflation, and this can also have a big effect on prices. You have no control over these things, so you must watch trends in the market and situations in the world to determine what percentage of spot market price you are willing to pay.

When you are in the gold business, it pays to watch the news. You must also consider that, at least in most cases, the gold you get from your customers is not pure gold; it is mixed with alloys. You will occasionally see gold bullion or gold coins, but mostly you get karat gold in the form of jewelry. European-made jewelry will be marked with the percentage of pure gold contained in the piece instead of a karat mark (k) like American jewelry. Here is a listing of karat marks and corresponding European marks and percentages of pure gold:

U.S.A.	European	Percentage
24k	999	99.9
18k	750	75
14k	585	58.5
l0k	417	41.7
8k	333	33.3

I have seen a lot of 22k gold jewelry that was brought back by servicemen which they bought while on deployment. These pieces are sometimes marked as 90 percent, or 900. There is also dental gold (yes, people really do take the gold out of dead people's mouths), which is usually 16k or 65 percent gold.

Once you figure out what karat gold you are working with, you have to decide how much per pennyweight you want to pay for it. For example, a customer brings you a 10k yellow gold class ring with a red stone in it, and it weighs in at 10 dwt. The gemstones in 99 percent of all class rings are synthetic and are worth practically nothing for scrap. You must estimate the weight of the stone and deduct that amount from the total weight of the ring. If the stone weighs 1.5 dwt, then the gold in the ring weighs 8.5 dwt. Next, you will need to figure the price per dwt for 10k gold, which is 41.7% pure gold. $47.50 per dwt (the previously determined gold value for that day) times 41.7 percent equals $19.81 per dwt. This is the price per pennyweight you will receive from the refiner on the day he receives it from you if the spot price is $1000 per ounce. I will normally pay $9 to $10 per pennyweight for a ring like this. This works out to $77 to $85 to buy it. This leaves me room to still make a profit even if gold goes down in value.

I always try to buy jewelry at prices that enable me to make a profit at scrap. If I am able to sell a piece at retail/wholesale, then it's a big bonus. Retail jewelry can bring double or triple its scrap value. When you decide to send gold to a refiner for scrap, you should wait until you have at least 100 dwt. My refiner pays up to 95 percent of spot price on shipments over 100 dwt.

Most class rings are very difficult to sale as jewelry, so at the prices discussed earlier, I would receive about $168 ($19.81 x 8.5 = $168.39) for the class ring. I could make as much as a $91 profit on this ring. Here are some formulas to use when trading in gold:

Spot price of gold ÷ 20 dwt = spot price per dwt.

Spot price per dwt x karat percentage = karat price per dwt.

Karat price per dwt x 95 percent = price per dwt from refiner.

I don't usually go through all these calculations. Instead, I rely on a table similar the one following unless I have a difficult customer who has had offers from other dealers and I must offer a better price.

10k $9 to $10 per dwt

14k $13 to $14 per dwt

18k $17 to $18 per dwt

22k $21 to $22 per dwt

24k $24 to $25 per dwt

Sterling Silver (925) 60 to 70 cents per dwt

or $12 to $14 per troy ounce

Platinum (90%) $21 to $22 per dwt

This price chart is just an example based on a spot price of gold at $1000 per ounce, silver at $30 and Platinum at $1000. You must make your own calculations to change your chart as the price of the metals goes up or down. I have been buying scrap gold for many years, and spot prices have varied from just under $300 per ounce to just over $1700 per ounce and silver from $4 to $50 per ounce. I have always used the same price ratios that are listed above, and I have always made a profit.

Testing for Fakes

It may look like gold, feel like gold, and even be marked with a karat mark, but it still may turn out not to be gold. Even after years of experience, I have been fooled.

With the new electronic gold testers that

are now on the market, testing gold is fast, easy, and accurate. The tester I have works by placing the piece to be tested on a tray and attaching an alligator clip, which is wired to the positive lead, to the piece. The negative lead is wired through a tube that contains a special gel. Twisting the back of this tube dispenses a drop of this gel, and the authenticity and karat value of the piece is tested by touching the drop of gel away from the point where the piece contacts the alligator clamp. You then press the test button to get a numerical reading, which is compared to a scale that gives you a karat value. This is a vast improvement over the old method of acid testing with a touch stone.

To acid test a piece of gold, you must have a file and some nitric acid. You must file into the piece to get through any layers of gold plating and then apply the acid to the bare metal. Gold will keep the acid clear,

34

silver will turn it yellow, and other metals will turn it green. To determine the karat value, the piece must be rubbed on a touchstone, acid applied, and the colors interpreted. These methods are time consuming and inaccurate. Even if you can file an area that won't be noticed, you will still leave an ugly mark on the jewelry. Some customers won't allow you to do this to their jewelry, which leaves you with the choice to either not take it or not test it.

For years, I got by without using an electronic tester, but if I had tested a few of the fakes I took, the tester would have easily paid for itself. Most of the time, I can tell that a piece is real, but if there is any question in my mind at all, I run it on my tester. I highly recommend that you buy an electronic gold tester and use it often until you gain enough experience to do without it. It is also a good idea to weigh the jewelry and reach an agreement with the customer for a price before you do your testing. After you've had enough experience, you will be able to tell the good from the bad about 99 percent of the time. Most gold-plated jewelry will be marked as such. Some of these markings are:

1/10 12k (14k, 18k, 24k) G.F.
1/20 12k (14k, 18k, 24k) G.F.
G.F.
Gold Filled
R.G.P.
Rolled Gold Plated
Heavy Gold Electroplate
10k, 14k, 18k, or 24k H.G.E.

When you see a piece marked 14kp or 18kp, it doesn't mean that it is plated, but that it is "plumb" gold. Plumb means that the gold content is exactly the karat marked. In 1976, Congress amended the National Gold and Silver Act, and by 1981, all American gold manufacturers had to adhere to the stricter standards for gold content in their jewelry. Previously, for example, jewelry manufacturers could mark their jewelry as 14k when it was actually only 13k. Since 1981, all American jewelry manufacturers have marked their jewelry with the plumb designation.

Sometimes you will encounter silver jewelry that is gold plated. This is also called gold overlay. This type of jewelry isn't usually marked as plated but is marked with the designation 925. This means the piece is 92.5 percent silver. Look for plated jewelry to show peeling and wear if it's been worn often. These things will show even better if you look at it closely with your loupe.

In my experience, gold chains are the items most often faked. Most gold chains are soldered on their ends, or, at the very least, the ring that attaches the clasp to the chain is soldered. While this isn't always proof positive that you have the genuine article, it is a good indicator. I have taken fake chains that look real even to the soldered ends.

When I took them in, I failed to test them with my acid (I didn't have an electronic tester at the time). They were marked 14k, and they had nice lobster-claw clasps on them, but they were not gold. They were evidently gold-plated brass that was made specifically to rip off people like me who buy gold. This lesson was enough to convince me to buy an electronic gold tester. From then on, any piece of jewelry that doesn't look right and every chain, get checked on my electronic gold tester. If you are not well acquainted with jewelry, it is in your best interest to check most everything that comes to you until you are confident that you can spot fakes. Even then, you will want to check anything that looks suspicious in any way. It only takes a loss on one fake to cancel out the profit on several good deals.

Deficit spending is simply a scheme for the 'hidden' confiscation of wealth. Gold stands in the way of this insidious process. It stands as a protector of property rights.
Alan Greenspan

Chapter 3

• •

Gemstones

Don't gain the world and lose your soul, wisdom is better than silver or gold...
Bob Marley

Diamonds conjure up visions of wealth and beauty. They inspire awe and mystery in people. Most people consider them to be the most valuable objects in the world, but diamonds are nothing but rocks, mere pieces of stone. When cut and polished correctly, they are things of beauty, but there is nothing mysterious or magical about them. The fact that they are valuable and expensive is a testament to the public relations campaign put on by the De Beers diamond cartel. I won't get into the saga of the De Beers family or a history of the

39

diamond industry, but it is sufficient to say they are responsible for making the diamond what it is today.

At one time, the De Beers controlled 90 percent of the world's diamonds, either in their own vaults or in the countries where the world's diamonds are produced. By controlling supply and, through continuous commercial campaigns, this diamond cartel has kept the price of diamonds artificially high. Everyone knows diamonds are forever, diamonds are a girl's best friend, and that if a man loves a woman he must give her a diamond. The De Beers have convinced us that diamonds are extremely rare, when in reality they are only rare because the diamond cartel strictly controls supply. As the De Beer diamond cartel fades, the price of diamonds will probably fall close to the price of rubies, sapphires, and emeralds.

In the meantime, you can make large amounts of money buying and selling diamonds. There is no spot market or London fix for diamonds like there is for gold. You can't check the TV or the local newspaper for a daily quote on the price of diamonds.

The price of diamonds is affected by the famous four "Cs." These are carat, color, clarity, and cut. Of course, the price of a raw uncut diamond is only affected by the last three Cs, but you will likely never see a raw diamond, so I will explain the basics about finished diamonds. The basics should be enough to get you started, but I recommend that you do some reading and research. It would take volumes to teach everything about this subject.

Let me first deal with what a carat is. Notice that it is spelled with a "c" and not a "k." Diamonds are weighed in carats, and the content of gold in a piece of jewelry is measured in karats. It is not necessary to buy a scale to weigh diamonds, because most times you will be dealing with mounted stones, and you can only estimate the weight if the stone is attached to a ring. It would be convenient to have a carat scale to weigh loose stones, but I have always gotten by without one. A carat is broken down into points so that 1 ct equals 100 pts. The corresponding fractional carats are also broken down into points. These are:

7/8 ct = 85 to 90 pts

3/4 ct = 75 pts

3/5 ct = 60 pts

1/2 ct = 50 pts

3/8 ct = 40 pts

1/3 ct = 33 pts

1/4 ct = 25 pts

1/5 ct = 20 pts

1/8 ct = 12 pts

1/10 ct = 10 pts

Color

The next thing to consider is color.

42

Diamonds come in several colors besides white. I have seen diamonds as blue as sapphires, as brown as rusty water, as green as emeralds, and as yellow as sunflowers. These are usually called fancy-color diamonds, and they can be worth more than their counterpart, which is white. Most of the stones I see that have color are not fancy colored but just off color. This is not a good thing. I always pay less for off color diamonds. The closer a diamond is to being colorless the better. I'm sure you've heard of diamonds being blue/white. This doesn't mean the diamond has a blue tint but that it is nearly colorless. Color can have a big effect on the value of a diamond, maybe even more than the other Cs. The Gemological Institute of America (GIA), an appraiser's association, rates the color of diamonds on a scale from D through Z+.

Clarity

The third factor to consider when buying

diamonds is clarity. When diamonds were formed thousands of years ago, most of them trapped small particles of carbon inside. These flaws look like tiny pieces of coal, air spaces, fractures, or small feathers.

If no flaws can be seen with a 10X loupe, then the diamond is said to be flawless. There is really no such thing as a flawless diamond, because if you have a strong enough microscope, flaws can be seen in every diamond.

Cut

The final C is cut. The way a diamond is cut can mean the difference between a brilliant sparkle of reflected light and a dull fish-eye appearance. The cut of a diamond probably has the least effect on its price but is still an important factor. Modern faceting machines are now used to cut diamonds, but fallible men run them. There are precise specifications for every style of diamond cut, but these measurements are often impossible for the diamond cutter to achieve. The diamond cutter tries to end up with the largest stone he can get from a raw diamond, but he must also try to cut off any flaws he can. Sometimes the result is less than perfect and can affect the value of the stone.

Evaluating Diamonds

There is a standard procedure I use to evaluate a diamond ring to be sold. I check the karat marking and weigh the piece to determine its gold value. If the mark is difficult to read, I use my 10X loupe. With my loupe still at hand, I use it and my diamond gauge to estimate the approximate weight of the stone. By holding the gauge over the diamond, looking at it through my loupe, and moving the gauge until I find the hole that the diamond completely fills, I can make a fairly accurate guess on the weight of the stone. The stone must completely fill the hole, leaving no space around the edge.

45

The gauge gives readings in points. Occasionally, I get a ring that is marked inside with its weight in points. When I find this, it gives me a good idea of how accurately I'm estimating the weight of diamonds using my gauge. When a ring has more than one diamond, I estimate the weight of each one, and then add these together for a total weight. Sometimes it's hard to get the gauge right on top of small diamonds, so I get as close as possible or sometimes next to the stone and compare the stone to the holes and take a guess. I find that in most cases, diamonds in clusters have even sizes like 1/4 ct, 1/2 ct, 1 ct, etc.

When I look at a stone with my loupe, I also check for flaws and damage. Always check very carefully for damage, especially around the girdle of the stone. The girdle is the part of a diamond that is easiest to damage. This area is very thin, and people chip their diamonds through abuse or neglect and never even realize they've done it. I have also seen chips in diamonds that occurred either before or during mounting and were hidden under a prong. A diamond that is chipped is worth considerably less than one of equal quality that is not chipped. A severely chipped diamond can be almost worthless.

Severely included diamonds are also something to watch out for. In the past couple of years, I've seen more of what I call "promotional diamonds." These are really trashy stones of such poor quality that they look like cut and polished gravel. They are usually cut in countries where labor is extremely cheap. I base the amount given for them mainly on the gold weight. I rarely find diamonds that don't have some kind of flaw, and I can't ever recall getting any diamonds that meet the GIA criteria for a flawless rating. I usually figure that minor flaws in stones smaller than 20 pts have little effect on value. When the stone is larger than 20 pts, flaws start to make a big difference.

I also make a judgment about the cut and color of a diamond while estimating its weight and looking for flaws. These are difficult qualities to appraise unless you've been to GIA School. To check the color of a diamond, place a piece of white paper behind it, and look at it under good natural light.

How Much to Pay for Diamonds

The value of a diamond increases geometrically according to its size, not arithmetically. For example, a 1-ct diamond could be worth four times as much as a 1/2-ct diamond of equal quality instead of twice as much, even though it is only twice as large. I use a pricing scale similar to the one shown below:

Weight	Price
1 pt to 20	$.10 to $.25 per pt
20 pts to 25 pt	$.25 to $.50 per pt

25 pts to 50 pts	$.50 to $1 per pt
50 pts to 75 pts	$1 to $2 per pt
75 pts to 100 pts	$2 to $3 per pt 100
pts and larger	$2 to $5 per pt

(More for a stone larger than 2 ct)

These prices are, of course, for individual stones and not for the total weight of a cluster. For example, a customer has a ladies' 25-pt solitaire engagement ring that weighs 1 pennyweight. The stone has a few specks of carbon but is cut well and appears to be near colorless. I offer the customer $30 to buy it. (Before handing over the cash, check the stone on the diamond tester by touching the diamond with the probe on the tester while holding the ring.) I could scrap the mounting for $28.

The stone should bring at least $25 and I should be able to wholesale the ring for as high as $90. If the ring had a cluster of five stones that had the same total carat weight and the mounting weighed 1 dwt, I would

49

The Beginner's Guide to Gold and Silver Scrap

offer $17.50 to buy it. The mounting should scrap for $28, the stones $10 to $12 and wholesale about $50. Keep in mind that unlike gold mounting which can be sent off to a smelter, you would have to find your own buyer for the stones

When it comes to larger diamonds like 1/3 ct, ½ ct, 3/4 ct, 1 ct, and larger, your knowledge of diamonds becomes more important.

Buy all diamonds as cheaply as you can. The bottom has fallen out of the market for small diamonds and it is hard to get much for them as scrap. Small single cut diamonds (called "Melee") are virtually worthless as scrap. The last offer I had from a wholesaler for 3 or 4 carats of small diamonds was about 25 cents per point. Unless you need them for repairs it is hardly worth the time and effort necessary to remove them. Larger diamonds have declined in value also. Until you are good at judging the four "C's" then buy as low as you can.

Dismounting Diamonds and Gem Stones

When dismounting diamonds, you must be extremely careful not to chip or otherwise damage them when removing them from their mountings. You will need a ring clamp, needle-nose pliers, and a jeweler's saw.

Rings with Tiffany-style four- or six-prong mountings are easy to remove. Tightly clamp the ring in the ring clamp and, using the pliers, carefully pry the prongs away from the diamond. Gold is a soft metal and bends fairly easily, so you don't have to be Arnold Schwarzenegger to bend it. When the diamond becomes loose, dump it into a small Zip lock bag. Be careful not to drop it on the floor, because once on the ground, diamonds are very hard to find. I have dropped several small diamonds around my jewelry bench and never found them.

Diamonds mounted in other ways usually have to be cut out with a jeweler's saw. If you are going to scrap a ring, don't worry about tearing it up to get the diamond out. Just be concerned about damaging the diamond. The saw blade won't cut the diamond, although the diamond will dull the blade in a hurry. Try to cut only the metal holding the diamond in the mount. I sometimes find it helpful to use an engraving tool with a flat point to finish cutting the stones loose. If you have a large stone you want to scrap but are afraid to cut it out of the mounting, Bluestone Trading the buyer I list in the Appendix will take it out for you and pay you for the scrap. Bluestone will pay 97% for the scrap gold mounting. Currently, most scrap diamond buyers are not much interested in smaller diamonds. They are almost always interested in stones that are 1/3 ct and larger.

Be sure to use your diamond tester before buying any diamonds. It is really embarrassing to send a diamond off for scrap only to be informed that it is a fake.

RUBIES, SAPPHIRES, AND EMERALDS

When buying gold jewelry with rubies, sapphires, or emeralds in them, I don't add much over the price of the gold in which they are mounted. The reason is that it hard to find a buyer for these stones as scrap, and I value jewelry more for its scrap gold value than its artistic value. Don't get me wrong, these are rare and desirable gems, and they are salable as jewelry, but they must be acquired cheaply to be profitable. There are also a lot of fakes out there. A diamond can be tested on a diamond tester, and gold can be tested on a gold tester, but colored gems are hard to authenticate. You almost have to be a gemologist to distinguish the real from the fake colored gemstones.

53

Evaluating Colored Gems

I use my diamond gauge to size colored gems, but the holes in it do not give an accurate estimate of their weight, because they are calibrated for diamonds. Colored gems are weighed in carats, but a carat of diamonds is different from a carat of colored gems. Like a diamond, the weight of a colored gem has an effect on its value, and its value tends to grow geometrically with its size. In my opinion, though, size doesn't make a difference until a gem weighs more than half a carat. I also think emeralds are worth about 10 percent more than both rubies and sapphires. Burma and Thailand dump tons of rubies and sapphires on the world markets every year. Most of the world's emeralds come from South America and seem to be much rarer.

The four Cs that apply to diamonds are also important to the value of colored

54

gemstones. Color is very important. After all, they are colored gems. The color of gems can be enhanced by heat and chemicals, and this is another good reason not to put too much money into them. As far as clarity goes, it is better to have a few flaws in a colored gem, because this can be an indication of its authenticity. Man-made gems can be made with flaws but generally are not. As far as cut goes, it has the least effect on the gem's value. Most all the colored gems I've seen lately are cut in Asia where the labor is cheap. These are, for the most part, pretty good stones, but I have seen some slop. Carat weight, of course, is also a factor.

How Much to Pay for Colored Gems

A good rule is to never pay more than actual gold price for piece of jewelry with colored stones in it. To me, buying these colored gems is like shooting craps. You put your money down, roll the dice, and take your chances. But there is good money to be made if you get a good piece for a low price. If you can buy jewelry with colored gems actual gold value in it, then it would be hard to lose money. For example, I purchased an emerald ring that had a large, carat-sized, emerald-cut emerald with diamonds on each side and it was mounted in an 18k gold ring. The diamonds tested as real and weighed about 25 pts total. The 18k gold mounting weighed over than 2 dwt. The emerald had a nice green color to it and a few small visible flaws. It appeared to be real—I'd seen many man-made emeralds and their color was usually darker. At today's gold prices I would offer $75.00. There was that much gold in the ring so it would be hard to lose money. This ring was taken to local appraiser, who estimated the ring's value at more than $1,000. Needless to say, I was very happy.

There is good money to be made with these colored gems, but until you have gained experience, be careful. Don't worry about a customer walking away because you made a low offer. Normally, you can buy these pieces for your price, and there will be someone else right behind the customer who walked away who is willing to sell to you.

OTHER STONES

Stones like topaz, pearls, opals, and amethyst are valued mainly for the gold in their mountings or the diamonds around them. You will see the large quartz type stones like topaz and amethyst mounted in 10k and 14k rings. Some of these stones can be more than an inch wide and quite heavy. These pieces should be purchased mainly for their gold, and the approximate weight of the stone should be deducted. Generally, if the stone is smaller than the largest ring in my diamond gauge, I will not deduct its weight. If it is between that size and the size of a dime, I will deduct 1 or 2 dwt. If the stone is larger than a dime, I will deduct 3 or 4 dwt. For instance, if the ring weighs 10 dwt, and the stone weighs 3 or 4 dwt, you should only pay for 5 or 6 dwt.

If the stones are smaller and look attractive, I will usually count them as part of the gold weight. Or, if the amount I come up with is a dollar or two short of an even number, I will usually add enough to make a round number. For instance, if I have a ring with an opal that weighs enough to give $18, I will usually offer an even $20 if I think I can sell the ring as jewelry.

I always buy these rings at prices that allow a profit if they must be scrapped. If they look nice enough, I will try to sell them first because I can usually get about twice their scrap value this way. Any rings that have a scratched or damaged stone will almost always wind up in the scrap pile.

SELLING JEWELRY

Look online for what diamonds and

diamond jewelry is selling for. Take a look at Wal-Mart, Sam's Club and any other discount outlets in your area. If want to sell jewelry then you will have to compete with Craig's List, EBay and the discount stores. If you buy right then you should be able to offer better prices. People are willing to pay a more to established sellers and retail outlets. You need an established clientele that trust you before you will be able get top dollar for your used jewelry. Check out local Jewelers and Pawn Shops in your area. Jewelers that have survived the latest recession and the increase in gold prices should be selling at good prices. Some will be buying gold and silver themselves but many will be interested in items you may want to sell. Find a jeweler who will sell on consignment if you don't have your own store front. Find an honest jeweler and develop a good relationship so you can have your items repaired. Most jewelers will give you dealer prices for repairs if you bring them lots of work just to keep their goldsmiths busy.

I have had great success over the years selling used jewelry to friends, co-workers, neighbors and family. Since you will also be buying from these same folks, the trick is not to offer them the same jewelry you that bought from them. Develop a network of other dealers like yourself that will take your jewelry for consignment and sell it in different markets, that way there is less risk of selling a rerun. This same network can be a source of consignments that you can sell or you can make jewelry trades to vary your inventory.

Finally remember to trade fairly and honestly with folks. Your good reputation will be an asset to your business. Follow all the laws and pay your taxes.

If you are truthful you will have as much gold as you want. Greek proverb

Appendix

Laws Governing Precious Metals Dealers in Virginia

These are the current regulations concerning Precious Metals Dealers in the State of Virginia. Look up the laws that in your state to see what you will need to do the buy scrap gold and silver in your state. There may also be other local laws. I'm sure there are some states and localities that do not require licenses or otherwise regulate buying precious metals scrap but every place will have laws about buying stolen goods. If you buy stolen goods then you are considered to be a "Fence" and the local constabulary will happily prosecute you to the full extent of the law. DO NOT BUY STOLEN GOODS. That being said, most people will stay under the radar if you buy few pieces of jewelry from your friends, neighbors and coworkers. Gold and silver coins are usually exempt from scrap dealers'

61

laws. I'm no Lawyer but I believe the Virginia law also exempts Retail Jewelers and Goldsmiths but I would still comply with law.

§ 54.1-4100. Definitions.
For the purposes of this chapter, unless the context requires a different meaning:
"Coin" means any piece of gold, silver or other metal fashioned into a prescribed shape, weight and degree of fineness, stamped by authority of a government with certain marks and devices, and having a certain fixed value as money.
"Dealer" means any person, firm, partnership, or corporation engaged in the business of (i) purchasing secondhand precious metals or gems; (ii) removing in any manner precious metals or gems from manufactured articles not then owned by the person, firm, partnership, or corporation; or (iii) buying, acquiring, or selling precious metals or gems removed from manufactured articles. "Dealer" includes all employers and principals on whose behalf a purchase is made, and any employee or agent who makes any purchase for or on behalf of his employer or principal.
The definition of "dealer" shall not include persons engaged in the following:
1. Purchases of precious metals or gems directly from other dealers, manufacturers, or wholesalers for retail or wholesale inventories, provided that the selling dealer has complied with the provisions of this chapter.
2. Purchases of precious metals or gems from a qualified fiduciary who is disposing of the assets of

an estate being administered by the fiduciary.

3. Acceptance by a retail merchant of trade-in merchandise previously sold by the retail merchant to the person presenting that merchandise for trade-in.

4. Repairing, restoring or designing jewelry by a retail merchant, if such activities are within his normal course of business.

5. Purchases of precious metals or gems by industrial refiners and manufacturers, insofar as such purchases are made directly from retail merchants, wholesalers, dealers, or by mail originating outside the Commonwealth.

6. Persons regularly engaged in the business of purchasing and processing nonprecious scrap metals which incidentally may contain traces of precious metals recoverable as a by-product.

"Gems" means any item containing precious or semiprecious stones customarily used in jewelry.

"Precious metals" means any item except coins composed in whole or in part of gold, silver, platinum, or platinum alloys.

(1981, c. 581, § 54-859.15; 1988, c. 765.)

§ 54.1-4101. Records to be kept; copy furnished to local authorities.

A. Every dealer shall keep at his place of business an accurate and legible record of each purchase of precious metals or gems. The record of each purchase shall be retained by the dealer for at least twenty-four months and shall set forth the following:

1. A complete description of all precious metals or gems purchased from each seller. The description shall include all names, initials, serial numbers or other identifying marks or monograms on each item purchased, the true weight or carat of any gem, and the price paid for each item;

63

2. The date, time and place of receiving the items purchased;

3. The full name, residence address, work place, home and work telephone numbers, date of birth, sex, race, height, weight, hair and eye color, and other identifying marks;

4. Verification of the identification by the exhibition of a government-issued identification card such as a driver's license or military identification card. The record shall contain the type of identification exhibited, the issuing agency, and the number thereon; and

5. A statement of ownership from the seller.

B. The information required by subdivisions 1 through 3 of subsection A of this section shall appear on each bill of sale for all precious metals and gems purchased by a dealer, and a copy shall be mailed or delivered within twenty-four hours of the time of purchase to the chief law-enforcement officer of the locality in which the purchase was made.

(1981, c. 581, § 54-859.16; 1986, c. 316; 1988, c. 765; 1990, c. 783; 1991, c. 174.)

§ 54.1-4101.1. Officers may examine records or property; warrantless search and seizure authorized.

Every dealer or his employee shall admit to his place of business during regular business hours the chief law-enforcement officer or his designee of the jurisdiction in which the dealer is located or any law-enforcement officer of the state or federal government. The dealer or his employee shall permit the officer to (i) examine all records required by this chapter and any article listed in a record which is believed by the officer to be missing or stolen and (ii) search for and take into possession any article known to him to be missing, or known or believed by him to have been stolen.

(1991, c. 174.)

§ 54.1-4102. Credentials and statement of ownership required from seller.

No dealer shall purchase precious metals or gems without first (i) ascertaining the identity of the seller by requiring an identification issued by a governmental agency with a photograph of the seller thereon, and at least one other corroborating means of identification, and (ii) obtaining a statement of ownership from the seller.

The governing body of the locality wherein the dealer conducts his business may determine the contents of the statement of ownership.

(1981, c. 581, § 54-859.17; 1986, c. 316; 1988, c. 765.)

§ 54.1-4103. Prohibited purchases.

A. No dealer shall purchase precious metals or gems from any seller who is under the age of eighteen.

B. No dealer shall purchase precious metals or gems from any seller who the dealer believes or has reason to believe is not the owner of such items, unless the seller has written and duly authenticated authorization from the owner permitting and directing such sale.

(1981, c. 581, § 54-859.18; 1988, c. 765.)

§ 54.1-4104. Dealer to retain purchases.

A. The dealer shall retain all precious metals or gems purchased for a minimum of ten calendar days from the date on which a copy of the bill of sale is received by the chief law-enforcement officer of the locality in which the purchase is made. Until the expiration of this period, the dealer shall not sell, alter, or dispose of a purchased item in whole or in part, or remove it from the county, city, or town in which the purchase was made.

B. If a dealer performs the service of removing

precious metals or gems, he shall retain the metals or gems removed and the article from which the removal was made for a period of ten calendar days after receiving such article and precious metals or gems.

(1981, c. 581, § 54-859.19; 1988, c. 765.)

§ 54.1-4105. Record of disposition.

Each dealer shall maintain for at least twenty-four months an accurate and legible record of the name and address of the person, firm, or corporation to which he sells any precious metal or gem in its original form after the waiting period required by § 54.1-4104. This record shall also show the name and address of the seller from whom the dealer purchased the item.

(1981, c. 581, § 54-859.20; 1988, c. 765.)

§ 54.1-4106. Bond or letter of credit required of dealers when permit obtained.

A. Every dealer shall secure a permit as required by § 54.1-4108, and each dealer at the time of obtaining such permit shall enter into a recognizance to the Commonwealth secured by a corporate surety authorized to do business in this Commonwealth, in the penal sum of $10,000, conditioned upon due observance of the terms of this chapter. In lieu of a bond, a dealer may cause to be issued by a bank authorized to do business in the Commonwealth a letter of credit in favor of the Commonwealth for $10,000.

B. If any county, city, or town has an ordinance which regulates the purchase and sale of precious metals and gems pursuant to § 54.1-4111, such bond or letter of credit shall be executed in favor of the local governing body.

C. A single bond upon an employer or principal may be written or a single letter of credit issued to cover all employees and all transactions occurring at a single location.

(1981, c. 581, § 54-859.21; 1988, c. 765.)

§ 54.1-4107. Private action on bond or letter of credit.

Any person aggrieved by the misconduct of any dealer which violated the provisions of this chapter may maintain an action for recovery in any court of proper jurisdiction against the dealer and his surety. Recovery against the surety shall be only for that amount of the judgment which is unsatisfied by the dealer.

(1981, c. 581, § 54-859.22; 1988, c. 765.)

§ 54.1-4108. Permit required; method of obtaining permit; no convictions of certain crimes; approval of weighing devices; renewal; permanent location required.

A. No person shall engage in the activities of a dealer as defined in § 54.1-4100 without first obtaining a permit from the chief law-enforcement officer of each county, city, or town in which he proposes to engage in business.

B. To obtain a permit, the dealer shall file with the proper chief law-enforcement officer an application form which includes the dealer's full name, any aliases, address, age, date of birth, sex, and fingerprints; the name, address, and telephone number of the applicant's employer, if any; and the location of the dealer's place of business. Upon filing this application and the payment of a $200 application fee, the dealer shall be issued a permit by the chief law-enforcement officer or his designee, provided that the applicant has not been convicted of a felony or crime of moral turpitude within seven years prior to the date of application. The permit shall be denied if the applicant has been denied a permit or has had a permit revoked under any ordinance similar in substance to the provisions of this chapter.

C. Before a permit may be issued, the dealer must have all weighing devices used in his business inspected and approved by local or state weights and measures officials and present written evidence of such approval to the proper chief law-enforcement officer.

D. This permit shall be valid for one year from the date issued and may be renewed in the same manner as such permit was initially obtained with an annual permit fee of $200. No permit shall be transferable.

E. If the business of the dealer is not operated without interruption, with Saturdays, Sundays, and recognized holidays excepted, the dealer shall notify the proper chief law-enforcement officer of all closings and reopenings of such business. The business of a dealer shall be conducted only from the fixed and permanent location specified in his application for a permit.

(1981, c. 581, § 54-859.23; 1986, c. 316; 1988, c. 765.)

§ 54.1-4109. Exemptions from chapter.

A. The chief law-enforcement officer of a county, city or town, or his designee, may waive by written notice implementation of any one or more of the provisions of this chapter, except § 54.1-4103, for particular numismatic, gem, or antique exhibitions or craft shows sponsored by nonprofit organizations, provided that the purpose of the exhibitions is nonprofit in nature, notwithstanding the fact that there may be casual purchases and trades made at such exhibitions.

B. Neither the provisions of this chapter nor any local ordinances dealing with the subject matter of this chapter shall apply to the sale or purchase of coins.

C. Neither the provisions of this chapter nor any local ordinance dealing with the subject matter of this chapter shall apply to any bank, branch thereof, trust company or bank holding company, or any wholly owned subsidiary thereof, engaged in buying and selling gold and silver bullion.

(1981, c. 581, §§ 54-859.24, 54-859.27; 1984, c. 583, § 54-859.28; 1988, c. 765.)

§ 54.1-4110. Penalties; first and subsequent offenses.

A. Any person convicted of violating any of the provisions of this chapter shall be guilty of a Class 2 misdemeanor for the first offense. Upon conviction of any subsequent offense he shall be guilty of a Class 1 misdemeanor.

B. Upon the first conviction of a dealer for violation of any provision of this chapter, the chief law-enforcement officer may revoke the dealer's permit for one full year from the date the conviction becomes final. Such revocation shall be mandatory for two full years from the date the conviction becomes final upon a second conviction.

(1981, c. 581, § 54-859.25; 1988, c. 765; 2010, c. 100.)

§ 54.1-4111. Local ordinances.

Nothing in this chapter shall prevent any county, city, or town in this Commonwealth from enacting an ordinance regulating dealers in precious metals and gems which parallels this chapter, or which imposes terms, conditions, and fees that are stricter, more comprehensive, or larger than those imposed by this chapter. In any event, the terms, conditions, and fees imposed by this chapter shall constitute minimum requirements in any local ordinance. Any fee in excess of the one specified in § 54.1-4108 shall be

reasonably related to the cost of enforcement of such local ordinance.
(1981, c. 581, § 54-859.26; 1988, c. 765.)

He who has the Gold rules, until someone shows up with a gun. **Anonymous**

Associations

National Pawnbrokers Association
P. O. Box 508
Keller, Texas 76244
Phone: 817-337-8830
Email: info@NationalPawnbrokers.org

Internet: www.nationalpawnbrokers.org
Or http://pawnindustrymarketplace.com
(This is an excellent source for links to gold refiners, silver buyers, jewelry supplies, diamond dealers and other wholesale buyers.)

Books

The following is a list of books that I use and that I highly recommend acquiring.

Beyond the Glitter: Everything You Need to Know to Buy, Sell, Care For, and Wear Gems and Jewelry Wisely
Gerald L. Wykoff
(This is the best book ever written on this subject. It is well written, easy to

understand and is full of need to know knowledge. I believe it may now be out of print but it is still available at Amazon, Ebay or your local Library.)

Or

Beyond the Glitter (Gemology I, Vol. 1)
Gerald L. Wycoff GG CSM Ph.D
(I have not seen this material but I assume it contains the same information that his book does.)
Available online at Amazon and others.

Blue Book of U.S. Coins - Paperback
Whitman Publishing, LLC
3103 Clairmont Road

Suite B
Atlanta, Georgia 30329
800-546-2995
Available online at Amazon and others.

The Official Blackbook Price Guide to United States Coins
Random House, Inc
1745 Broadway
New York, NY 10019
212-782-9000
Available online at Amazon and others

(You can probably get by with either of the above. Most of the coins I see are culls but occasionally a collectable coin with extra numismatic value will show up.)

71

Coin Dealers Newsletter "Grey Sheet"
CDN
P.O. Box 7939
Torrance, CA 90504
http://greysheet.com
Email: orders@greysheet.com
(This is a wholesale newsletter for Coin Dealers.)

Diamond Buyers

Bluestone Trading Company
P.O. Box 24126
Cleveland, Ohio 44124
440-442-7280
888-800-BLUE
Fax: 440-442-0026
        800-321-7979

(I have dealt with Bluestone trading for many years and I have found them very honest. I do not list other diamond buyers because I have had no dealings with any other but there are several others listed at the NPA Pawn Industry website.)

Gold and Silver Refiners, Scrap Buyers

Garfield Refining Company
810 East Cayuga Street

Philadelphia, PA 19124

Tel: 800-523-0968

Fax: 215-533-5902

Email: info@garfieldrefining.com

www.garfieldrefining.com

Hoover and Strong

10700 Trade Road

Richmond, Virginia 23236-3000

1-800-759-9997

Fax: 1-800-616-9997

www.hooverandstrong.com

(Hover and Strong has an excellent tutorial and chart online at;

http://www.hooverandstrong.com/category/ Buying+Jewelry+Scrap)

Kitco Logistics, Inc.

64 Lake Street

Rouses Point, NY 12979

1-888-259-7227

1-518-297-2300

Fax: 1-518-297-2301

www.kitco.com

Midwest Refineries, LLC
4471 Forest Ave.
Waterford, Michigan 48328
1-800-326-2955
Fax: 1-248-674-7305
www.midwestrefineries.com

(I have done business with the above refining companies. There are more listed at the NPA Pawn Industry website.)

Jewelry Supplies and Tools
National Jeweler's Supply
101 Mystic Ave
Medford, MA 02155
888-657-8665
www.nationaljewelerssupplies.com

Polishers & Jewelers Supply Corp.
662 Atwells Ave.
P.O. Box 3448
Providence, RI 02909
Tel: 1-401-454-2888
Fax: 1-401-454-2889
www.pjsupply.com

Silverware Buyers

Beverly Bremer Silver Shop
3164 Peachtree Road N.E.
Atlanta, GA 303005
1-800-270-4009
1-404-261-4009

Although the author of this book has made every effort to ensure that the information in this book was correct at press time, the author does not assume and hereby disclaims any liability to any party for any loss, damage, or disruption caused by errors or omissions, whether such errors or omissions result from negligence, accident, or any other cause.

Warning!

**The next pages you read may have
eternal consequences.**

I have found that money, possessions, gold and silver did not fill the God shaped hole in my soul. True happiness is not found in wealth. I realized that one day I would die and all the gold and silver that I had acquired would stay above ground and my body would go underground. We work all our lives to dig wealth up, only to leave it and be buried ourselves. There is only one thing that filled me up, Jesus Christ. I have found the Peace that only he can provide. I highly recommend that everyone seek him. By confessing my sins and receiving him into my heart, I now have eternal life. That is something that all the gold and silver in the world or the power they can buy, cannot provide. Jesus Christ, his cross and his blood are the only way to Father God and eternal life with him. I still have gold and silver but I do not put my faith in it, I put my faith in God. I have been investing in his Kingdom and my investment will be waiting for me when I see him. The Bible says a lot about gold, silver, money, investing and how we should use them, pick up a copy and read it. Find a good bible centered Church and give your life to Yeshua Jesus our Messiah. It will be the best investment you will ever make.

God Bless

V Alexander Cullen